D1012941

DISCARD

Fallen Angels

Yale University Press

New Haven & London

Angels

Harold Bloom

Illuminations by

Mark Podwal

Designed by Nancy Ovedovitz and set in Mrs Eaves by Tseng Information Systems, Inc. Printed in Italy by EuroGrafica SPA.

Library of Congress Cataloging-in-Publication Data

Bloom, Harold.

Fallen angels / Harold Bloom ; illuminations by Mark Podwal.

p. cm.

ISBN 978-0-300-12348-7 (alk. paper)

1. Devil. 2. Devil in literature. I. Podwal, Mark H., 1945–

II. Title

BL480.B56 2007

202'.16—dc22   2007022156

A catalogue record for this book is available from the British Library.

♾ The paper in this book meets the guidelines for permanence and durability of the Committee on Production Guidelines for Book Longevity of the Council on Library Resources.

10 9 8 7 6 5 4 3 2 1

Contents

Illuminations

Fallen Angels

or three thousand years we have been haunted by images of angels. This long literary tradition extends from ancient Persia through Judaism, Christianity, Islam, and the various American religions. With the approach of the millennium, our obsession with angels intensified. But these popular angels were benign, indeed banal, even insipid. The 1990s saw the publication of many books on angels—on contacting and communicating with guardian angels, on angelic intervention, healing, and medicine, on angelic numbers and oracle cards—there were even "angel kits" (one can only imagine). *The Present Darkness* (1986) and its sequel, *Piercing the Darkness* (1989), which depict the struggles between demons and angels in the fictional college town of Ashton, were among the biggest sellers in the so-called Christian fiction genre: *The Present Darkness* has sold in excess of 2.5 million copies. *A Book of Angels,* by Sophy Burnham, published by Ballantine Books in 1990, was a *New York Times* best seller and one of the books often credited with starting the publishing bonanza of angelology. According to the publisher, the book "tells not only the extraordinary true stories of present-day encounters with angels, but also traces the understanding and study of angels throughout history and in different cultures. What do angels look like? Whom do they choose to visit? Why do they appear more often to children than to adults? An eloquent report from the place where earth and heaven meet, *A Book of Angels* is a quest into mysteries and a song of praise to life." The popular *Angelspeake: How to Talk with Your Angels* (1995), by Barbara Mark and Trudy Griswold, offers a "practical" guide for readers. The decade saw, too, the release of any number of movies whose main characters were angels; to name just a handful, *Wings of Desire* (1988), *The Prophecy* (1995), *Michael* (1996), *Meet Joe Black* (1998), and *Dogma* (1999). There were also angel T-shirts, mugs, calendars, postcards, jewelry, and sunglasses. Nor, on evidence of a quick Amazon search, has the angel craze abated in any significant way since the passing of the millennial year. To cite just a few recent books: *Contacting Your Spirit Guide*

(2005), *Angels 101: An Introduction to Connecting, Working, and Healing with Angels* (2006), and *Angel Numbers* (2005; a pocket guide to "angelic meanings of numbers from 0 to 999").

There are also popular obsessions with fallen angels, demons, and devils, who are only rarely insipid. The star figure among them, Satan, began as what we now would call "a literary character" long before his apotheosis in the *Paradise Lost* of John Milton. I had better explain precisely what I mean by that beginning, since so many people confuse problems of literary representation with the very different questions of belief and disbelief. One can provoke considerable abuse by the truthful observation that the Western worship of divine beings is grounded in several distinct but related instances of literary representation. The

Yahweh of the J writer, first of Hebrew authors, is certainly an astonishing literary character, conceived with a shrewd mingling of high irony and authentic awe. The Gospel of Mark's Jesus may not be the first literary portrait of Mary's son, but certainly it has proved the most influential. And the Koran's Allah is palpably a literary monologist, since his voice speaks all of the book, in tonalities that convey a comprehensive personality.

Demons belong to all ages and all cultures, but fallen angels and devils essentially emerge from a quasi-continuous series of religious traditions that commence with Zoroastrianism, the dominant world religion during the Persian empires, and pass from it to Exilic and post-Exilic Judaism. There is a very ambivalent transference

of bad angels from later Judaism to early Christianity, and then a quite ambiguous transformation of the three earlier angelic traditions into Islam, difficult to trace precisely because Neoplatonic and Alexandrian systems like Hermetism get into the mix.

To most of us, the fallen angel proper is Satan, or *the* Devil, whose early literary history is very much at variance with his ongoing status as a celebrity. The book of Job, a work of uncertain date, seems to me quite as surprising a presence in the canon of the Hebrew Bible as are Ecclesiastes and the Song of Songs. Job's book begins when an angel called the *satan,* who seems to be God's prosecuting attorney, or accuser of sin, enters the divine court and makes a wager with God. The satan is one of the "sons of God," in good standing, while the Hebrew word *satan* means an obstructer, someone who is more a blocking agent or stumbling block than an adversarial force. Neil Forsyth, whose book on Satan, *The Old Enemy* (1987), remains unsurpassed, points out that "the Greek for 'stumbling block' is *skandalon,* which gives us not only 'scandal' but also 'slander.'" This first or Jobean Satan appears to be God's CIA director and becomes very bad news for poor Job. Forsyth traces Satan's downward path through the book of the prophet Zechariah, where Yahweh reprimands Satan for an abuse of power but does not remove him from his office as Accuser.

The Hebrew Bible thus has the word *satan* but absolutely does not have Satan him-self—fallen angel, devil, and chief of de-mons. Satan proper, who became crucial to

Christianity, was not a Jewish but a Persian idea, invented by Zoroaster (Zarathustra) more than a thousand years before the time of the historical Jesus. Demons, of course, are universal—every culture, each nation, all peoples had them from the start—yet Zoroaster went well beyond Iranian notions of demons when he fashioned Angra Mainyu, later to be called Ahriman, the Spirit of Evil. Energetic in evil, Ahriman was God's twin brother, which is distinctly not an idea that Christianity extended to its version of Ahriman, the New Testament's Satan. Who after all would have been the father who begot both God and Satan? There are esoteric traditions that make Satan Christ's twin brother; ultimately that is a return to Zoroaster's vision. Satan—the greatest blend of fallen angel, demon, and devil—disturbs all of us because we sense how intimate a relation we enjoy with him. The Romantics are frequently blamed for that enjoyment, but I think it is older than Romanticism and touches deep elements within us, though the Romantics, and Lord Byron in particular, can be credited for having enhanced these elements.

I suspect that all of us, almost whoever we are, have richly ambiguous attitudes toward the idea of "fallen angels," and rather less so toward that of "devils," let alone "demons." We don't necessarily take it as an insult when someone says to us, "You devil you," or calls us "a devil of a fellow," or even "a she-devil." Sometimes we uneasily accept being called a "demon," particularly when the reference is to the intensity of our energies. Yet I don't know many, in literature or in life, who are not rather charmed by being described as "a fallen angel." "Fallen angels," though theologically identical with "devils" and sometimes with "demons," retain a pathos and a dignity and a curious glamour. Somehow the modifier does not cancel out the substantive; however fallen, they remain angels. T. S. Eliot tended to blame this upon John Milton, and once referred to Milton's Satan as a curly-haired Byronic hero. Though that was a silly description of *Paradise Lost*'s tragic villain, it accurately reflected a cultural identification that persuaded the nineteenth century and still leads a kind of underground existence.

George Gordon, Lord Byron, was and is *the* Fallen Angel proper. His various imitators, ranging from Oscar Wilde to Ernest Hemingway and Edna St. Vincent Millay, have never been able to displace him. The Brontë sisters, fiercely in love with the image of Byron, provided better imitations of him in Emily's Heathcliff and Charlotte's Rochester. English rock stars, not always consciously, frequently are parodies of the noble Lord Byron, and so of course are hosts of film stars. Byron was superbly ambiguous in his narcissism: incestuous, sadomasochistic, homoerotic, and famously fatal to women. His notorious charisma emanated from his self-identification as a fallen angel: he is Manfred, Cain, Lara, Childe Harold—all versions of the Miltonic Satan. Byron's enormous vogue throughout Europe and America was vastly stimulated by his heroic death at thirty-six, attempting to lead Greek brigands in their revolt against the Turks. But his death, life, and poems together probably did not match in notoriety his popular role as the most seductive of all fallen angels.

In his wonderful satire *The Vision of Judgement,* Byron gave an engaging portrait of Satan:

> But bringing up the rear of this bright host
>   A Spirit of a different aspect waved
> His wings, like thunder-clouds above some coast
>   Whose barren beach with frequent wrecks is
>   paved—
> His brow was like the Deep when tempest-toss'd—
>   Fierce and unfathomable thoughts engraved
> Eternal wrath on his immortal face—
> And *where* he gazed a gloom pervaded Space.

That is clearly a rather cheerless but not undignified fellow, and, like most Satanic representations in Byron's projects, Byron himself. His devils are not jolly, like Mephistopheles in Marlowe's *Dr. Faustus* and Goethe's *Faust,* but they are always noble, like Lord Byron, who never allows his readers to forget the high birth of their poet. Demons and devils generally are not exactly noble, but fallen angels are almost never vulgar or plebeian. Benign angels all too often seem to confuse their innocence with ignorance, but fallen angels always seem to have enjoyed an old-fashioned education and a proper upbringing. Byron was very much a Regency dandy and snob, and he may have inspired the visual tradition in which fallen angels tend to outdress the unfallen, who are frequently naked anyway.

There is, as I keep noting, a fundamental duality of response that most of us experience in regard to all three of those dangerous entities: fallen angels, demons, and devils. They provoke in us both ambivalence and a certain ambiguity of affect. This mingled delight and horror is more ancient than Romanticism, and more universal than Western tradition. Ibsen, himself at least half a troll, gave us grand trolls in Brand, Hedda Gabler, Solness the Master Builder, and several more, and a half-troll in Peer Gynt. Rather reluctantly, Ibsen followed Shakespeare, whose Puck overtly is an English troll but whose great villains—Iago, Macbeth, the Edmund of *King Lear*—are more demonic and trollish than at first seems wholly compatible with being human. But that is part of Shakespeare's invention of the human, to teach us the extent to which many of us are more fallen angels than devils. Hamlet, who is his own Falstaff, is also to a surprising degree his own Iago, and Hamlet has become a paradigm for all of us. Is Hamlet a fallen angel? Are we fallen angels? Both questions could be dismissed as non-sense, yet they have their reverberations.

Presumably the unfallen angels spoke (and speak) Hebrew, since Talmud and Kabbalah alike insist that God spoke Hebrew in the act of Creation, and what language would he have taught angels other than Hebrew? Fallen angels notoriously are polyglot, and sometimes they have turned into human beings. We know that Enoch began as a mortal and then was transmogrified into the great angel Metatron, who in Gnostic and Kabbalistic traditions was known as the lesser Yahweh, more than an angel and almost co-ruler with God. Our father Jacob became Uriel, Emerson's favorite angel, and then the angel Israel. The fierce prophet

opposite: Unfallen Angels Spoke (and Speak) Hebrew

Elijah went up to heaven in a chariot of fire, and on arrival metamorphosed into the angel Sandalphon. Dissident Franciscans proclaimed that their great founder, Francis of Assisi, was no mere saint but the angel Rhamiel. The process goes both ways, and always takes us back to Adam, perhaps higher than the angels when he began, certainly lower than the angels when he fell, but where does he rank in comparison to fallen angels?

The center of any discussion of fallen angels has to be Adam, who seems to me a far greater fallen angel than Satan. Even as an imaginative idea, angels matter only if we matter, and we are (or were) Adam. Lest feminists disagree, I remind all of us that Talmud and Kabbalah alike argue that Adam originally was androgynous, as was his prototype, God. Adam, Enoch, Metatron,

opposite: Elijah's Metamorphosis

and God may be the same figure, a formulation that seems purely Mormon or Gnostic Kabbalistic but that Moshe Idel convincingly traces back to very early speculations, perhaps to an archaic Judaism itself, before even the J writer, or Yahwist, retold the story of Adam and Eve more or less as we have it since. The apotheosis of Enoch into Metatron is a return of Adam, interpreted by Kabbalah as the original God-Man, a fusion beyond the limits of our imaginations. Certain Gnostics spoke of the Angel Christ as being the restored Adam, a vision that opposes Saint Paul, since the Angel Christ is not a Second Adam but the true form of the First Adam.

Again, I am less concerned here with the angel Adam than with his fallen status. We can be fallen angels without being demons or devils, and I therefore want to see what light we can gain by recognizing this. Angels—unfallen or fallen—make sense to me only if they represent something that was ours and that we have the potential to become again. The people we call schizophrenics once were called angels; perhaps they still should be, which certainly does not imply that mental illness is a myth, or that cures for such illness ought not to be found. *Otherness* is the essence of the angels; but then it is our essence also. That does not mean that the angels are our otherness, or that we are theirs. Rather, they manifest an otherness or potential akin to our own, neither better nor worse but only gradated to a different scale. The Vatican Museum collects angels; piety and self-interest join in that concern. What the Vatican and the

American Religion alike would not accept is my increasing conviction that *all* angels, by now, necessarily are fallen angels, from the perspective of the human, which is the Shakespearean perspective. Every angel is terrifying, wrote the poet Rilke, who had not confronted a screen upon which John Travolta cavorted as an angel.

What can it mean to contend that no distinction is still possible between unfallen and fallen angels? We are fallen Adam (or fallen Eve and Adam, if you prefer), but we no longer are fallen in the Augustinian or traditional Christian sense. As Kafka prophesied, our one authentic sin is impatience: that is why we are forgetting how to read. Impatience increasingly is a *visual* obsession; we want to see a thing instantly and then forget it. Deep reading is not like that; reading requires patience and remembering. A visual culture cannot distinguish between fallen and unfallen angels, since we cannot *see* either and are forgetting how to read ourselves, which means that we can see *images* of others, but cannot really see either others or ourselves.

omentarily set aside your probable skepticism, and assume with me that we *are* fallen angels, a larger category in my view than devils or demons. In a popular reduction, we frequently feel that little children are angels, reflecting Victorian conventions. Since we grow up, we fall, or, more simply, are fallen. But that is a little too simple, since our current American obsession with angels is rather more childish than childlike. The ancient angels did not fall because they grew up, though that is certainly one version of the Satanic argument.

C. S. Lewis, eminent defender of ortho-
doxy, argued just the reverse: the angels who
fell were those who failed to mature. William
Empson, in his *Milton's God,* disagreed with
the angelic C. S. Lewis by observing that
God himself provoked Satan's rebellion.
Saint Augustine, alas, has to be our ultimate
authority upon the Fall: *The City of God,* Augustine's masterwork, says that Satan and his
cohorts fell through pride, which seems to
me very different from immaturity.

I blame Augustine for causing much of
Western desperation by his insistence that
Satan's fall took place *before the creation of Adam.*
Augustine's most original (and pernicious)
idea is that because we fell with Adam and
Eve, we are always guilty and sinful, disobe-
dient and lustful. I myself agree with the
Gnostics, who said that we fell when we, and

the angels, and the cosmos, were all created simultaneously. On the Gnostic account, which became also the Kabbalistic and Sufi stories, there never were unfallen angels or unfallen men and women or an unfallen world. To come into separate being was to have fallen away from what the orthodox called the original Abyss but the Gnostics called the Foremother and Forefather. The angel Adam was a fallen angel as soon as he could be distinguished from God. As a latter-day Gnostic I cheerfully affirm that we are all fallen angels, and I turn now to dividing us off and away from our nastier cousins, the demons and devils.

Demons are universal, and belong to all peoples of all eras. Ancient Mesopotamia was particularly overrun by demons: spirits of the wind, they could gain entry every-

where, and they showed a fierce obsession with ruining human sexual harmony. The star demoness was Lilith, who later re-appeared as Adam's first wife in Talmudic and Kabbalistic tradition. Driven out by the creation of Eve, Lilith flew off to the cities of the Levantine coast, and continued her career as the sexual temptress beyond all others. Though Babylonia was particularly demon-ridden, our demonic heritage is endless. Ancient India, which saw demons everywhere, set the dreadful precedent of demonizing the dark-skinned peoples who were in possession of the North when the Indic invaders arrived. Egypt, in the earliest recorded times, associated all change with demons; night could not fall, or a year end, without demonic agency. With old age, illness, and death regarded as demons by

all cultures, we might wonder how the demonic ever achieved the curious ambiguity
accorded it by many Western traditions.

Today we remember the second-century
writer Apuleius for his Hellenistic masterwork, the splendid narrative called *The Golden
Ass.* Historically Apuleius is more impor-
tant for an essay, "On the God of Socrates." "God" there means Socrates' daemon,
a spirit that mediated between Socrates and
the divine. According to Apuleius, the daemons have transparent bodies and hover in
the atmosphere, and so can be heard but not
seen. Though transparent, the daemons are
material, and some, like the daemon of Socrates, are benign, representing our genius.
As a good Neoplatonist, Apuleius believed
that each of us has an individual daemon,
a guardian spirit. In an oddity of cultural

history, these amiable daemons, who included the spirits of sleep and love, became associated by medieval Christian theologians with *demons,* or badly fallen angels, such as Saint Paul's "prince of the power of the air." A curious split has existed now for a thousand years, in which many Christians see the "daemonic" and the "demonic" as being one and the same. That is doubly unfortunate, in my judgment, because the daemon is our genius, in the aesthetic and intellectual senses, and to mix up our gifts with the terrible universe of death is a disaster. But the other aspect of the misfortune is even darker: we may all of us be, as I suggest, fallen angels, but our guardian spirit or daemon protects us, as it did Socrates, from the worst moral consequences of our fall. To compound daemon with demon is to place ourselves in an unnecessary jeopardy.

Yet that in turn brings me to the third category of this discussion: devils. The Devil proper is Satan, and I return to him now in his New Testament role and his subsequent literary and experiential career. There are a remarkable number of Satans, and I want to distinguish between the principal figures lumped together under this most lurid of names. When and where did he first go bad, or at least acquire the blame for not less than everything? Not in the Hebrew Bible, as we have seen, where he remains an instrument of God. But in the book of Chronicles, Satan rather ambiguously seems to act independent of God, when King David blunders and enforces a census, at Satan's stimulation and supposedly against God's will. In Jewish Apocryphal and Apocalyptic literature, particularly the books of Enoch, a full transition begins to the book of Jubilees, where

Satan appears under the name of Mastema, though even in Jubilees the status of Mastema is not fully defined. The Dead Sea Scrolls name Satan as Belial and for the first time identify him with radical evil, wholly in rebellion against God. We are on the verge of Satan's truly independent career, which finds rival evaluations in Gnostic and Christian accounts. Just as there is no single origin of Satan, there is no definitive story about him. Shakespeare's Iago and Milton's Satan cast a backward glow upon the Satan of the ancients, who is in many ways a far less imaginative conception than he was to become fifteen hundred years later.

I am afraid that the Satans of the four Gospels are essentially what we now term instances of anti-Semitism. The authors of the Gospels place identifications of Satan and the Jewish people in the mouth of Jesus, and these vicious travesties have done vast harm to the Jews and to the authentic Jesus, whoever you take him to have been. The Jesus portrayed in the Gospel of John is particularly egregious in these attacks upon "the Jews," but Jesus is not my subject here. Satan or the Devil is, but I question whether the canonical Gospels of the New Testament actually afford us any coherent vision of Satan. Essentially, the Satan of the Gospel authors is a metaphor comprehending all Jews who will not accept Jesus as the Messiah.

Saint Paul, whose writings precede all four Gospels, is not much interested in demons. That leaves us with the Revelation of Saint John the Divine, whose Satan is more central, but as a cosmological principle. The New Testament frequently alludes to Satan but almost never confronts him. Milton, in his great epic *Paradise Lost,* truly invented the

literary Satan whom I admire most, in his
first speech, when he awakens in Hell:

If thou beest he; but O how fallen! how changed
From him, who in the happy realms of light
Clothed with transcendent brightness didst
    outshine
Myriads thought bright: if he whom mutual league,
United thoughts and counsels, equal hope
And hazard in the glorious enterprise,
Joined with me once, now misery hath joined
In equal ruin: into what pit thou seest
From what highth fallen, so much the stronger
    proved
He with his thunder: and till then who knew
The force of those dire arms? Yet not for those,
Nor what the potent victor in his rage
Can else inflict, do I repent or change,
Though changed in outward lustre, that fixed mind
And high disdain, from sense of injured merit,
That with the mightiest raised me to contend,
And to the fierce contention brought along

Innumerable force of spirits armed
That durst dislike his reign, and me preferring,
His utmost power with adverse power opposed
In dubious battle on the plains of heaven,
And shook his throne. What though the field be
    lost?
All is not lost; the unconquerable will,
And study of revenge, immortal hate,
And courage never to submit or yield:
And what is else not to be overcome? [1.84–109]

William Blake observed that Milton was of the Devil's party without knowing it, and this superb oration manifests enormous imaginative sympathy, on the poet's part, with Satan's heroic stance. Shelley in a sense was accurate when he ironically remarked that the Devil owed everything to Milton, though he also could have given a share of the credit—if that is the right word—to Saint Augustine.

he Hebrew Bible has no
fallen angels since they
are not a Judaic idea.
The Satan of the Book
of Job is a prosecuting
attorney, an official of God
in perfectly good standing. In Isaiah 14:12–
14, when the prophet sings the fall of the
morning star, the reference is to the king
of Babylon and not to a fallen angel. There
is a similar Christian misreading of Ezekiel
28:12–19, where the prince of Tyre falls
from his position of "the covering cherub,"
or guardian, of Eden and is cast out by God.
Despite Shelley's wit, I would say that the
Devil's true debt was to Saint Augustine,

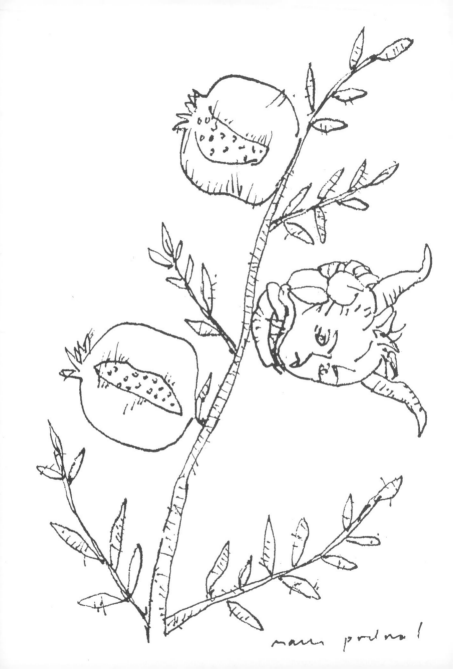

Christian theologian of the fourth century of our Common Era, who is doubtless the greatest of all Christian thinkers. What we might call the Christian Satan is central to the *City of God,* in which we are given the story of Satan's rebellion, caused by his pride and crushed before the creation of Adam, so that Satan's subsequent seduction of Adam and Eve is secondary to the fall of the angels. Augustine also invented the very original idea, totally un-Judaic, that Adam and Eve were created by God in order to replace the fallen angels. It is by the fall of Adam and Eve that we all are eternally guilty and sinful. Only Christ can save us from that guilt.

emons and the Devil— or devils—are more interesting in literary and visual contexts than they are in what remain the canonical texts of Christian faith. Even Augustine has no interest in the individuality of Satan; for Augustine, Satan is, above all, *useful,* a point upon which he insists he follows Paul. I myself am loyal to the sublime Oscar Wilde, who was always right and who insisted that all art was perfectly useless. If you are the kind of dogmatic Christian who more or less follows Paul and Augus-

tine, then Satan now is more than useful to you—you *need* him. But if your interests are primarily aesthetic, then Satan will matter to you only where he has been supremely represented, as he was by John Milton. And Satan mattered to Milton only because the idea of fallen angels humanly mattered. I go back again to my central contention: if we ourselves are Satanic, that is mostly because we share Satan's dilemma of what it means to be a fallen angel. Hamlet, as always, phrases matters best: "What a piece of work is a man, how noble in reason, how infinite in faculties, in form and moving, how express and admirable in action, how like an angel in apprehension, how like a god! The beauty of the world; the paragon of animals; and yet to me what is this quintessence of dust?"

"How like an angel in apprehension":

for Shakespeare, "apprehension" begins as a sensory perception, but then becomes an imaginative mode of anticipation. Hamlet, far more than Byron's heroes, is clearly a fallen angel; Horatio envisions flights of angels singing the prince to his rest. In Hamlet—as in even the best among us—the fallen quality is dominant, yet the angelic apprehension always abides. That returns us to the perpetual fascination of the idea of angels: are we a mockery of them, or do they suggest to us, as they did to Hamlet, something godlike about the human imagination, with its apprehension of something evermore about to be? The anticipation that, in exalted moments, seems to stand tiptoe in us is an angelic mode of apprehension. Even if angels have always been metaphors of human possibilities either unrealized or thwarted, we need to understand better what it is that these metaphors intimate.

Orthodox accounts of angels tend to enforce too rigorous a distinction between the fallen and unfallen, and thus also make angels too alien for us fully to comprehend. These days, in our country, many of us are silly about angels and mindlessly spot them everywhere. There isn't much difference in the popular mind between John Travolta playing an angel or playing President Clinton: one quasi-cherub seems as good as the other. Metaphorically and humanly, it seems to me a great loss to either estrange or debase the idea of an angel. One of the most powerful (and ambiguous) of angelic encounters is the all-night wrestling match fought between Jacob and a nameless one among the Elohim, or sons of God. I give the biblical text here in the King James, or Authorized, Version:

And he rose up that night, and took his two wives, and his two womenservants, and his eleven sons, and passed over the ford Jabbok.

And he took them, and sent them over the brook, and sent over that he had.

And Jacob was left alone; and there wrestled a man with him until the breaking of the day.

And when he saw that he prevailed not against him, he touched the hollow of his thigh; and the hollow of Jacob's thigh was out of joint, as he wrestled with him.

And he said, Let me go, for the day breaketh. And he said, I will not let thee go, except thou bless me.

And he said unto him, What *is* thy name? And he said, Jacob.

And he said, Thy name shall be called no more Jacob, but Israel: for as a prince hast thou power with God and with men, and hast prevailed.

And Jacob asked *him,* and said, Tell *me,* I pray thee, thy name, And he said, Wherefore *is* it *that* thou dost ask after my name? And he blessed him there.

And Jacob called the name of the place Peniel: for I have seen God face to face, and my life is preserved.

And as he passed over Peniel the sun rose upon him, and he halted upon his thigh.

In Protestantism, the story of "wrestling Jacob" is interpreted as a loving struggle between God himself and Jacob. Ancient Jewish authorities, starting with the prophet Hosea, tended to identify that nameless "man" as an angel. Jacob's new name, Israel, frequently was interpreted as the "man who saw God," God somehow being credited with helping Jacob in the struggle to hold off the angel until dawn. Neither the Protestant nor the normative Jewish reading seems adequate to me. A contest that cripples you for life hardly seems very loving, and Jacob fights altogether alone, his will against the will of the nameless angel.

Who is that angel, who fears the break of day? Some early commentators nominated Metatron, while others (with whom I more nearly agree) gave the role to Sammael, the angel of death. Jacob, who fears that he will be murdered by his wronged half-brother, Esau, the very next day, ambushes the angel and lets him go before the first light; receives the blessing of the new name, Israel; and so himself becomes an angel, according to later esoteric texts. I am unorthodox or Gnostic enough to point out that the Jacob portrayed by the Yahwist or J writer is a wily trickster, a survivor generally more distinguished for cunning than for cour-

age. Indeed, his astonishing and desperate courage in ambushing the angel of death is so persuasive only because he does not truly change when he receives the angelic blessing. A kind of fallen angel when he is Jacob, he remains a fallen angel when he becomes Israel. Clearly, I have divested the Pauline-Augustinian adjective *fallen* of nearly all its theological meanings, so that for me a fallen angel and a human being are two terms for the same entity or condition.

What after all is the relationship between the angelic and the human? Saint Augustine assured us that everything visible in our world is under the supervision of an angel. That assurance does not distinguish between good and bad angels, and I increasingly am reluctant to make such a distinction. Milton's Satan manifests a superb

consciousness until Milton, clearly nervous about his epic protagonist, systematically debases him in the final quarter of *Paradise Lost*. That is the aesthetic difference between Milton and Shakespeare, since we are never allowed to reject our dramatic sympathy for Iago.

Milton, very much in the spirit of the Hebrew Bible, seems to have understood implicitly that angels were not a Jewish invention but rather returned from Babylon with the Jews. Angels, ultimately Zoroastrian, emerge from a vision that sees all reality as an incessant war of good and evil. Shakespeare's vision, far subtler, sees each of us as her or his own worst enemy, for reasons having little or nothing to do with good and evil.

Hamlet's angelic apprehensions help

destroy him because they teach him that we can find words only for what is already dead in our hearts. Able to think like an angel, Hamlet thinks too well, and thus perishes of the truth, pragmatically becoming a version of the angel of death. Hamlet is death's ambassador or messenger to us, and though his message is endlessly enigmatic, it has established itself as universal. Part of that message is that the angelic and the human are virtually identical, yet this is not a happy equivalence. The combat with the angel in Prince Hamlet does not yield the blessing of more life, though ironically it does grant Hamlet a new name. I say "ironically" because the name is still "Hamlet," but when we think of the name we think only of the Prince and not of his father, whom we know as the Ghost.

opposite: Sammael, the Angel of Death

Ibn Harabi, the great Sufi sage of thirteenth-century Andalusia, remarkably altered the biblical metaphor of Jacob's contest with the Angel. For Harabi, who followed Jewish mystical sources in this interpretation, it was better to speak not of a combat with or against the Angel but rather of a combat *for* the Angel, because the Angel cannot become a true self as form without the intercession of a human agonist. Clearly, Harabi's Angel is anything but a representation of death, and yet I want to adapt the idea of a combat *for* the Angel to my own purposes. Fallen angels, demons, and devils are merely fascinating grotesques if we cannot make any use of them for our own lives. We are neither Jacob nor Hamlet, though like Jacob we hope to hold off the angel of death, and like Hamlet we brood upon "the

dread of something after death, / The un-
discovered country, from whose bourn / No
traveller returns."

Our contemporary images of angels are
all mixed up with alien visitations, whether
in the benign fantasy of *Close Encounters of the
Third Kind* or in the self-destructive fantasy
of the Heaven's Gate cult. Images of a lost
transcendence haunt our popular culture.
Sometimes this nostalgia puzzles me because
we are a religion-mad nation, and if we truly
believed what we profess, then we would not
so wistfully pursue material evidences of
the spiritual world. But then I remind myself of my own favorite formulation, which
is that religion in America is not the opiate
but rather the poetry of the people. Angelicism is a populist poetry, and perhaps can
be partly redeemed from its sentimentalism

and its self-deception if we can find our own versions of "the combat for the Angel." In naming us all as so many fallen angels, I intend to suggest an approach to one of those versions.

e want demons and devils to entertain us, at rather a safe distance, and angels to comfort or look after us, again at a safe remove. But fallen angels can be uncomfortably close, since they are ourselves, in whole and in part. Our *Frankenstein* movies have given us a famous monster who simply does not exist as such in Mary Shelley's Romantic novel *Frankenstein, or the Modern Prometheus.* In that book, Franken- stein is the Promethean scientist who cre- ates not a monster but a daemon, who makes a remarkable appeal to his morally obtuse maker: "Oh, Frankenstein, be not equitable

to every other, and trample upon me alone, to whom thy justice, and even thy clemency, and affection, is most due. Remember that I am thy creature; I ought to be thy Adam, but I am rather the fallen angel, whom thou drivest from joy for no misdeed."

Mary Shelley's poignant sentences render the fallen angel another form of Adam, which seems to me exactly right. In relation to death, we once were the immortal Adam, but as soon as we became subject to death we became the fallen angel, for that is what the metaphor of a fallen angel means: the overwhelming awareness of one's mortality. Hamlet's angelic apprehensions are sharper intimations of mortality than are elsewhere available in imaginative literature. The dilemma of being open to transcendental longings even as we are trapped inside a dying animal is the precise predicament of the fallen angel, that is to say, of a fully conscious human being. Old age, illness, and death itself were regarded as demons in most of the world's traditions, and the doublet of "death and the devil" is one of the most famous of Christian phrases. Fallen angels, not in any ideological sense but as images of the essential human predicament, are far more central to us.

I think now that current American post-millennial obsession with what we call angels is mostly a mask for the American evasion of the reality principle, that is, the necessity of dying. There is very little difference between the so-called near-death experiences and the popular cultivation of the angels. Both near-death experiences and angelicism have been vigorously commercialized and remain growth industries. Deep reading conversely is in decline, and if we forget how to read and why, we will drown in the visual media. Fallen angels, as Shakespeare and Milton emphasize, should never stop reading. The sacred Emerson once remarked that all Americans were poets and mystics, and he is still accurate, even if their poetry and their mysticism is now all too frequently debased. But this is the Evening Land; our culture, such as it is, ebbs into twilight. The angel of Evening is at hand, fallen yet imbued with a final vitality. Is not the United States now such an angel? Knowingly to be a fallen angel is not the worst of conditions, nor the least imaginative.

Tony Kushner's *Angels in America* is prob-ably our most recent American instance of the sense in which all of us are fallen angels.

Kushner's angels have been abandoned by God and decide to sue him for desertion. Unfortunately for all of us, God retains the truly Satanic Roy Cohn as his defense attorney, and so the angels will lose their case. As a parable for our current situation, Kushner's vision is beautifully appropriate.

hat are the uses of a consciousness that involves some sense of being a fallen angel? My question is wholly pragmatic, as is my reply. Love and death, according to the Hermetic revelation, came into being together when the androgynous Divine Man first created something for herself or himself. What she created was a reflection of herself, seen in the mirror of nature. In that moment of creation/reflection we divided into men and women, and also we first fell asleep. Sleep and love thus were born together, and love engendered death. This Hermetic myth is

more than a touch disconcerting, but for me
it explains our fall far more adroitly than
Saint Augustine did. I would not call Shakespeare a Hermetist, as the late Dame Frances
Yates did, because Shakespeare contains
Hermetism as he contains everything else;
Hermetism cannot contain Shakespeare. But
I think that Hamlet regards the dilemmas
of love and death in a spirit more Hermetic
than either Christian or skeptical. Hamlet is
a fallen angel in the Hermetic sense; he has
learned that love, whether erotic or familial,
engenders death. "It is we who are Hamlet,"
William Hazlitt said. Our most creative im-
pulses thrust us further into a confrontation
with the mirror of nature, where we behold
our own image, fall in love with it, and soon
enough fall into the consciousness of death.
Though I call such angelicism "fallen," it is

the inevitable condition whenever we seek
to create anything of our own, whether it be
a book, a marriage, a family, a life's work. I
cannot urge you, or myself, to celebrate an
angelicism that so profoundly contemplates
the paradox that love engenders death.
And yet, that is the painful glory, or glorious pain, of our existence as fallen angels.
Call it *Yeziat,* "get thee out," Abraham from
Ur, Moses from Egypt, or Jacob *into* Israel,
Yahweh's Promised Land.